A Religio

# HOW TO FIND OUT WHAT (THE) GOD (OF YOUR UNDERSTANDING) WANTS FROM YOU

Rabbi Brian Zachary Mayer

Mandorla

© 2008 by Rabbi Brian Zachary Mayer

Mandorla Press, LLC

www.mandorlapress.com

All rights reserved. No part of this book may be reproduced or transmitted in any for or by any means, electronic or mechanical, without written permission from the author, except for the inclusion of brief quotations in a review.

Thank you.

Publishers Cataloguing-in-Publication

Mayer, Brian Zachary.

How to find out what (the) God (of your understanding) wants from you : a religion outside the box book / Rabbi Brian Zachary Mayer. -- 1st ed. -- Los Angeles : Mandorla Press, 2008.

p. ; cm.

ISBN: 978-0-9800234-0-4

1. Spiritual life. 2. Religious life. I. Title. II. Title: Religion outside the box.

BL624 .M39 2008
204.4--dc22

Mandorla

2007907763
2008

First edition, second printing
Designed, printed, and all that good stuff in the USA.

Buddha left a road map, Jesus left a road map, Krishna left a road map, Rand McNally left a road map. But you still have to travel the road yourself.

- Stephen Levine

# IV — How To Find Out What (The) God (Of Your Understanding) Wants From You

# TABLE OF CONTENTS

ACKNOWLEDGEMENTS — VII

INTRODUCTION — 1

GOD, YOUR LIFE, AND BOTH — 3
- (THE) GOD (OF YOUR UNDERSTANDING) — 3
- YOUR SPIRITUAL-RELIGIOUS LIFE — 4
- YOU & GOD: THEOPHANY — 7

THE BIBLE AND BEYOND — 11
- THE BIBLE — 11
- BEYOND THE BIBLE — 14
- RABBI BRIAN'S THOUGHTS — 21

TOWARDS A PERSONAL THEOPHANY — 23

YOUR OWN THEOPHANY — 29
- A SIMPLE SPIRITUAL-RELIGIOUS EXERCISE — 31
- PRAYER — 39
- ROLE-PLAYING — 51

(RABBI BRIAN'S ANSWERS) — 67

CONCLUSION — 107

# ACKNOWLEDGMENTS

I WOULD LIKE TO THANK:

- God.*

- You, the reader, for reading these words, for picking up a book like this, and for being open to taking your spiritual-religious life into your own hands.

- Jane, my better half, for her love and support. Emmett, my son, for gracing us with his love.

- My advisory group, my cheer-squad, my teachers, and everyone else who helped me get this stuff out of my head and into this book you are holding.

---

\* Each and every person has the right to define for themselves what they mean by this word. Consequently, I caution you about making too many assumptions about what it is that you think I mean by the fact that I am grateful to God for my opportunity to have written this book.

How To Find Out What (The) God (Of Your Understanding) Wants From You

# INTRODUCTION

**Religion-Outside-The-Box,** my rabbinate-ministry, is dedicated to empowering adults to develop their spiritual-religious lives regardless of denominational affiliation, spiritual-religious baggage, or theology.

I am very proud to present here some of the methods I've discovered in this book, **How to Find Out What (the) God (of Your Understanding) Wants from You.**

## A STORY...

I want to share with you a story that explains how I see my role in helping you develop your spiritual-religious life:

> Once upon a time, there was a scared soul lost in the forest. After days of walking as straight a path as one can possibly walk in a forest, this person came across another soul and pleaded, "Please, please...help me find my way out of this forest."
>
> The response was: "I am not certain I am not more lost than you are. But, I know this: The way that I came from does not lead out. Let us take hands and journey together."

So it is with us — you reading and me writing. "Let us take hands and journey together."

I'm here to be a guide and friend. I don't know exactly what you should be doing with your spiritual-religious life. But I have some ideas that I want to share with you. Ultimately, I don't get a vote and I'm never going to tell you that you have to believe or disbelieve certain things. We are talking about *your* spiritual-religious life, after all.

Thanks for traveling with me.

Rabbi Brian

# GOD, YOUR LIFE, AND BOTH

### (THE) GOD (OF YOUR UNDERSTANDING)

Your relationship with (the) God (of your understanding) and what you mean by the word God are up to you. I don't see it as my job to tell you what you should or ought to believe here. That's why I often write "(the) God (of your understanding)" where other people would just write "God."

Let me expand on this a bit….

Your ideas about the best type of cake in the world and my ideas about the best type of cake in the world might differ.

Your ideas about how to best spend a weekend and my ideas about how to best spend a weekend might differ.

Your ideas about God and my ideas about God might differ.

You might believe that God is external, omniscient (all-knowing), benevolent (all-good), and omnipresent (everywhere).

And, you might not.

It doesn't really matter in this book.

(I know that might seem a bit revolutionary, but, nonetheless, it's true.)

Regardless of what you might use the word God to mean, this book will help you in discovering *How to Find Out What (the) God (of your understanding) Wants From You.*

(Re-read that last sentence. It's important you understand it.)

## Your Spiritual-Religious Life

It is said that we live in four different worlds: the physical, the emotional, the intellectual, and the spiritual-religious. The first three are easy to identify. However, most folks get stuck when talking about the spiritual-religious world. And, they get stuck for good reasons.

We can define the spiritual-religious as that which is not comprised of matter, feeling, or thought. In other words: the spiritual-religious is not the physical, the emotional, or the intellectual. But, this definition as the absence or negation of other things, doesn't really help.

The spiritual-religious — like truth, beauty, and love — is very hard to categorize. Moreover and adding to the difficulty, the spiritual-religious often encompasses notions of God, the infinite, and that which cannot be defined.

In Biblical days, the spiritual-religious was characterized as being "like the wind" because it can't be seen, yet its impacts are evident.

While I don't have a perfect definition of the spiritual-religious, I can tell you that by creating a relationship to your spiritual-religious life, you will gain a greater sense of *connectedness* and *perspective* in your overall life.

I don't mean to suggest that people who lack understanding of their spiritual-religious lives fail to experience connectedness and perspective. I am suggesting that those of us who are not the proverbial captains of our own spiritual-religious ships may experience feelings of connection only sporadically — as hit and miss feelings — compared to those of us who have developed "religious-spiritual fitness."

Think of it this way: physically fit people are better able to handle physical activities and are healthier than those who are unfit. Similarly, those who have spiritual-religious fitness have a greater sense that they are loved by an *unending love* — and they have a better understanding of what that means.

Your spiritual-religious life is like singing. Most of us can sing, but few of us do it in public. Even fewer do it in public without embarrassment. I want to encourage you to develop your spiritual-religious voice so that you can — to use the words of the Psalms — "sing a new song to God."

## What is a Healthy Spiritual-Religious Life?

People with fully developed spiritual-religious lives feel that they are *a part of something rather than apart from everything*. They see *meaning* in places that others do not. The criticism leveled at them — for example, of being a dreamer in the face of reality — doesn't bother them. They have a sense of *hope* and of *purpose*.

Having a developed spiritual-religious life can bring a greater sense of *faith* and *surrender*. It makes people *less frantic* and more able to *distinguish between things that can be changed and things that cannot*. Those with a healthy spiritual-religious life, are *calmer* — believing and knowing that *things work out in the grand scheme of things*. This belief and knowledge stays with them amidst the good and the difficult times.

People with developed spiritual-religious lives are better able to *accept things that are beyond their control*. They have the *courage* to change what needs to be transformed in their lives. They have a deeper *perspective* of the world. They see a glass of water as half-full, not half-empty. In fact, they can even see how one's attitude can turn a prison into a monastery (or vice versa).* Moreover, their perspective gives them the ability to sit through and move on from "negative" feelings — as opposed to sublimating them, denying them, and watching them appear elsewhere.

---

\* This is such a powerful notion that I want to repeat it here: one's attitude can turn a prison into a monastery, or a monastery into a prison.

Those with developed spiritual-religious lives feel connected to and have a meaningful relationship with (the) God (of their understanding).

And, you reading this book are — regardless of your denominational affiliation, past baggage, or theology — on your way to a healthy spiritual-religious life.

## You & God: Theophany

The word "theophany" comes from the Greek words *Theo* ("God") and *phainein* ("to show oneself"). Theophany means an appearance of or revelation by God. Theophany is related to the word "epiphany" which literally (and similarly) means a manifestation of God but has come to mean a leap in understanding.

The premier and classic example of a theophany is the encounter Moses had with the burning bush as recorded in Exodus 3 in the Bible.

I don't know anyone for whom God has appeared so clearly. And, I doubt that you either know anyone for whom this has happened or that you have had this type of experience yourself.

And, although people constantly hope to see a miracle that will give them the answers and direction they're searching for — it hardly ever works that way. (The) God (of your understanding) is not going to break character with your understanding of God — otherwise, (the) God (of your understanding) wouldn't be the God of your understanding. For example, if you don't believe that God would or could speak to you out of flaming shrubbery, you probably won't experience that type of theophany.

So, if (the) God (of your understanding) wouldn't alter reality in a dramatic way to give you messages, how might this communication occur?

That's the big question.

Some people, when they don't get revelation in a way they assume they should, substitute a reliable authority's notion of what God wants from them. (And there is nothing wrong with that — that is why we hire and respect experts.) There are plenty of organized religious traditions that espouse beautiful notions of what it is that God wants. (For example, in the Bible, in Micah 6:8, the answer of what it is that God wants is summarized as, "Do justice, love kindness, and walk humbly with your God.")

Another opinion regarding the apparent lack of God revelation of God's self in a burning bush is to assume that God doesn't mean to or care to make contact.

I don't think that's the case.

Wonderful other options exist.

And that's what this book is for — helping you *find out what (the) God (of your understanding) wants from you.*

You can have your very own theopany.

And, I'm going to show you how.

But before we do so, let me give you an overall tour of the rest of this book.

> **The Bible and Beyond** will explore some classical techniques people have used in divining the will of the divine.
>
> **Towards A Personal Theophany** will explore problems that occur in the absence of one official method of finding out God's will.
>
> **Your Own Theophany** will give you three specific spiritual-religious methods you can use to receive contact from (the) God (of your understanding).
>
> **(What The God Of Rabbi Brian's Understanding Wants From Him)** is a section in which I write what I think God wants from me with the hopes of getting you to think more about what (the) God (of your understanding) wants from you.

# THE BIBLE AND BEYOND

## THE BIBLE

Modern theologian Marcus J. Borg in his book *Reading the Bible Again for the First Time: Taking the Bible Seriously But Not Literally* makes a point I need to state here: to believe that the Bible is not the direct and inerrant word of God does not mean that there is no God. Moreover, to believe that there is no God doesn't mean that there is no value in examining the Bible.

(While the above might seem to be patently obvious, I know I felt freed-up after I read it.)

So, let's get that out of the way: belief in God and belief in the Bible aren't synonymous.

Nonetheless, at least in our culture, the two seem to be inextricably entangled.

In 2005, TIME Magazine published an article beginning with the words, "If you are interested in God's position on…[the subject matter in question] please proceed to…." Then they referenced a Biblical book and chapter.

People — including major media conglomerations — regard the Bible as a primary source for figuring out what God wants.

I believe the Bible is a wonderful source of learning about how people have understood God and that it answers for many the question of what it might be that God wants. Nonetheless, I don't believe it is the only or even the best source of divining God's will.

Let me present three questions that keep me from subscribing to the notion that the Bible is the definitive, authoritative storehouse of God's will:

> 1) Why hasn't God made much direct contact since the Bible was written?
>
> 2) Why isn't the Bible laid out as an answer book to the question of what God wants? — and why doesn't it proclaim itself to be the authoritative answer book explaining God's will?
>
> 3) Why do people in the Bible use methods other than the Bible to divine God's will?

The first question is traditionally answered by the devout with the following reasoning: if God made contact with us, this would negate the necessity of faith. (While on the surface it might seem a controvertible alternate explanation, I would also suggest that the answer might also be utilitarian: whoever has been given authority to interpret God's bestseller wields tremendous power in society.)

As for the second question, I've never heard a good explanation.

Regarding the third question — if the Bible is the only or best way to find out God's will, why do people in the Bible use other methods of divination? — no answer suffices. If divination by augury and austromancy work in the Bible, why should we not use them today? (You'll find out what augury and austromancy are on the next page.)

Please note: I have a lot to say about the Bible. (I'm working on a book explaining what it is, what it has been used for, what you need to know, and more.) I can't really go that much into the Bible in this document. Nonetheless, if you can understand the following, it will help a lot:

> Let me propose what might seem, at first, radical. There is a difference between TRUE and TRUTH. George Washington never took a hatchet to a cherry tree. (Most of us don't have a problem with that story not being true.)
>
> While it is not TRUE in an empirical sense — no reporter would have reported on it happening — it is still a TRUTH story. It is a story about TRUTH — or at least a truth that we would like to think is a cornerstone of this country (that lying is bad). While not true, the story still has a truth in it.

The same is true with the Bible. Perhaps you can see it as not being TRUE but about TRUTH? (Sit with that for a while.)

Moreover, there is a little known spiritual-religious concept known as *paradoxicality* — which again, we don't have the space here to go into. Paradoxicality, simply, is the ability to know that something that isn't true can also be true at the same time. For example, I don't beleive that I was a slave to Pharaoh in the land of Egypt, and yet I can beleive that I was as well. (More on this in future Religion Outside The Box books.)

## Beyond the Bible

Following is a list of divination methods to give you an idea of the breadth of choices you have when trying to figure out what God wants.

*This list is not meant to be read straight through, but to overwhelm you with options.* This list is here to underscore the premise that there is no one "right" way of finding out what (the) God (of your understanding) wants from you.

Methods of divination with the suffix -ology (such as genethlialogy — divination by the stars' placement at one's birth) have been omitted, as they are considered to be sciences and not methods of divination. (It's a fine line between the two.)

Methods directly referenced in the Bible as being legitimate methods of divination are so referenced with footnotes.[*]

---

[*] Spellings vary a lot. ◊ Sources include: answers.com, phrontistery.info, paralumun.com, themystica.com, paganforum.com, thewhitegoddess.co.uk.

| | |
|---|---|
| Aeromancy | Divination by atmospheric conditions |
| Alectryomancy | Divination by rooster |
| Aleuromancy | Divination by flour |
| Alomancy | Divination by salt |
| Alphitomancy | Divination by barley |
| Anemoscopy | Divination by wind |
| Anthropomancy | Divination by human sacrifice |
| Anthroposcopy | Divination by facial features |
| Apantomancy | Divination by animals |
| Arithmancy | Divination by numbers |
| Aruspicy | Divination by arrows* |
| Aspidomancy | Divination by trance from within a circle |
| Astragalomancy | Divination by dice (or bones) |
| Augury | Divination by the actions of birds† |
| Austromancy | Divination by wind and clouds |
| Axinomancy | Divination by axes‡ |
| Belomancy | (See Aruspicy) |
| Bibliomancy | Divination by books, especially the Bible (see Stichomancy) |
| Botanomancy | Divination by burning plants |

---

\* Ezekiel 21:21

† Isaiah 11:6 ◊ The day we brought my son home, an owl perched on the electric line behind our house. I'm certain it was a sign of something, I just don't know what.

‡ Psalm 74:5

| | |
|---|---|
| Brontoscopy | Divination by thunder |
| Capnomancy | Divination by smoke |
| Cartomancy | Divination by cards (see Taromancy) |
| Catoptromancy | Divination by mirrors |
| Causimomancy | Divination by burning |
| Cephalomancy | Divination by skulls |
| Ceraunoscopy | Divination by thunder and lightning |
| Ceremancy | Divination by wax into water |
| Chaomancy | Divination by aerial visions |
| Cheiromancy | Divination by palm inspection |
| Chirognomy | Divination by hands |
| Clairaudience | Divination by psychic hearing |
| Cleromancy | Divination by lots or by bones* |
| Cleidomancy | Divination by keys |
| Cometomancy | Divination by comet tails |
| Coscinomancy | Divination by hanging sieves |
| Critomancy | Divination by barley cakes |
| Cromniomancy | Divination by onion sprouts |
| Crystallomancy | Divination by crystals or other reflecting objects |
| Cybermancy | Divination via computer oracles |
| Cyclomancy | Divination by wheels |

---

\* Esther 9:24

| | |
|---|---|
| Dactylomancy | Divination by rings |
| Daphnomancy | Divination by burning laurel leaves |
| Demonomancy | Divination by demons |
| Empyromancy | Divination by burning |
| Eromancy | Divination by air and water |
| Exegesis | Divination by texts (especially those from the Bible)* |
| Extispicy | Divination by entrails of sacrifice† |
| Fortune Cookie | Divination by reading a message on a slip of paper in a baked cookie |
| Geloscopy | Divination by laughter |
| Gematria | Divination by the numerical value of letters in words |
| Geomancy | Divination by earth (including Feng Shui) |
| Gyromancy | Divination by dizziness |
| Haruspicy | (See Extispicy) |
| Hepatomancy | (See Extispicy) |
| Hieroscopia | (See Extispicy) |
| Hippomancy | Divination by horses |
| Hydromancy | Divination by water |

---

\* 2 Kings 22:8-13

† Leviticus 1:3 ff ◊ The point of having the priests do animal sacrifices in the ancient Near East was so that they could examine the dead animal and get a sense of God's will. (Some say the examination that Kosher and Halal butchers do to this day is a hold over from this ancient practice.)

| | |
|---|---|
| I Ching | Divination by use of 64 hexagrams |
| Icthyomancy | Divination by fish |
| Kephalonomancy | Divination interpreting the skull of a donkey |
| Lampadomancy | Divination by light |
| Lecanomancy | Divination by a basin of water |
| Libanomancy | Divination by incense |
| Lithomancy | Divination by precious stones |
| Logomancy | Divination by words* |
| Magic 8-Ball | Divination by a plastic toy manufactured by Mattel Inc.® |
| Margaritomancy | Divination by bouncing pearls |
| Meditation | Divination by non-thought thinking† |
| Metagnomy | Divination by visions |
| Meteormancy | Divination by meteors |
| Metoposcopy | Divination by foreheads |
| Moleosophy | Divination by blemishes |
| Myomancy | Divination by rodent behavior |
| Myrmomancy | Divination by ant behavior |
| Necromancy | Divination by the spirits of the dead‡ |
| Nephelomancy | (See Eromancy) |

---

\* Genesis 24:14
† 1 Kings 19:12
‡ 1 Samuel 28:8-12

| | |
|---|---|
| Nephomancy | Divination by clouds |
| Numerology | (See Arithmancy) |
| Oculomancy | Divination by eyes |
| Oinomancy | Divination by wine |
| Omphalomancy | Divination by umbilical cords |
| Oneiromancy | Divination by dreams* |
| Onimancy | Divination by oil and a young child |
| Onomancy | Divination by names |
| Onychomancy | Divination by fingernails |
| Oomantia | Divination by eggs |
| Ophiomancy | Divination by the color and movement of snakes† |
| Ornithomancy | Divination by birds of flight |
| Osteomancy | Divination by observing bones |
| Ovomancy | (See Oomantia) |
| Palmistry | (See Cheiromancy) |
| Pegomancy | Divination by spring water |
| Pessomancy | Divination by pebbles |
| Phyllorhodomancy | Divination by rose petals |
| Plastromancy | Divination by cracks inside a turtle's shell |
| Pyromancy | Divination by fire |
| Rhabdomancy | Divination by rods, wands, or sticks‡ |

---

\* Genesis 40:8

† Jeremiah 8:17

‡ 1 Samuel 23:9

| | |
|---|---|
| Rhapsodomancy | Divination by poetry |
| Scatomancy | Divination by droppings, usually from an animal |
| Sciomancy | Divination by shadows, spirits, or ghosts[*] |
| Sideromancy | (1) Divination by straw burning (2) Divination by stars[†] |
| Sortilege | (See Cleromancy) |
| Spodomancy | Divination by ash |
| Stichomancy | Divination by books or lines (see Bibliomancy) |
| Stolisomancy | Divination by clothing |
| Sycomancy | Divination by fig leaves |
| Taromancy | Divination by tarot |
| Tasseography | Divination by tea leaves or coffee grounds |
| Tephramancy | Divination by bark ashes |
| Tiromancy | Divination by cheese |
| Xylomancy | Divination by burning wood |

---

[*] 1 Samuel 28:7

[†] Isaiah 47:13

## Rabbi Brian's Thoughts

I doubt that God has ever tried to communicate with you through wine and cheese. (Nonetheless, attempting oinomancy and tiromancy at dinner parties might be fun.)

So, then, the question remains... how can you find out what (the) God (of your understanding) might want from you?

We'll explore just that in the next section...

But, while we are here in this parenthetical note, I want to take a moment to restate the importance of knowing what (the) God (of your understanding) wants from you. If you know what it is that God wants — howsoever you might conceptualize God — you will have better sense of calm, love, and purpose.

.

# TOWARDS A PERSONAL THEOPHANY

If there is no single, scientific or "right" way of knowing God's will, and you don't want to take someone else's word for it, then how are you supposed to know what (the) God (of your understanding) wants you to do?

Moreover, if (the) God (of your understanding) wouldn't alter reality in a dramatic way to give you messages, how might that communication occur?

For most of the people I have encountered, it seems those answers are within. And, this makes good sense. After all, if you were God and you wanted to make certain that all sentient beings were able to find their own sense of what they were looking for, where would you put the proverbial treasure if not within?

In other words, what (the) God (of your understanding) wants from you is what you know in your heart of hearts to be true — it's the stuff you know deep down you should be doing.

It's not always so easy to access that stuff, but that's most often what it is that (the) God (of your understanding) wants from you. What God wants of you is a personal thing, specific to you.

Let me write that again for emphasis:

> What God wants of you is a personal thing, specific to you.

Some folks get upset over this line of thinking. I don't quite understand why. Perhaps they perceive it as a threat to the hegemony of the organized religion they hold onto dearly. Let me assure these people that organized religion's walls are thick enough to keep it safe.

Other people get upset over this line of reasoning because they fear a society based on personal autonomy and personalized spiritual-religious practice would lead to relative morality. Sentiments like "I like chocolate" and "I will kill her for her possessions" would become of equal value. They aren't and they won't. (It always amazes me that many people who express this fear are the same people who profess to have so much faith in God — why are they so scared?) What we're talking about is you and what you do with your spiritual-religious life. You must still follow the laws of the community in which you live.

Finally, and not a lot of folks care about this one, the idea that God has wants is fraught with theological instability. After all, if God is perfect and/or unlimited, can God have wants? (This is addressed in the next section: *Theological Instability*.)

Here's justification that what God wants from you is something personal. First, according to Judaism, as long as you're older than 13 years, you are autonomous with regard to your spiritual-religious life. Moreover — and this is interesting no matter your family of origin

— spiritual-religious laws are typically divided into two categories: those between a person and his or her fellow persons, and those between a person and his or her own understanding of God. The former laws are about fitting into society. They are less open to interpretation. The latter set of laws — what's between you and (the) God (of your understanding) — is what we're talking about here.

Honestly, you probably already know a few things that God — however you choose to understand that — wants from you. It's as simple as doing those things you know you need to be doing — those things which, no matter how frequently you put them off, keep coming back to you.

Finally, let me go back to what I told you in the introduction and reiterate why it's important to know what God wants from you: *when you live a life doing things you know you're supposed to be doing, you will find yourself living with more meaning, fulfillment, purpose, and calm.* (There will still be struggles, of course, but your footing and resilience will be firmer.)

And, amazingly or not, it doesn't matter if you believe in God or not — or if God even exists. Doing what you *know* you're supposed do is satisfying.

## Theological Instability

It is a theologically unstable notion that an active, external God should have wants. If you think about it, if God is everywhere, capable of everything, and perfect, without lack — the idea that God could want something doesn't quite work. (You don't have to believe in a God who is everywhere, capable of everything, and perfect, without lack — I'm just pointing out the classical problem with this theology and the notion that God wants something from us.)

As I mentioned above, most folks don't really feel the need to explore this question.

Nonetheless, let me give one answer to this question of why would God want anything of us. The answer I am going to present is a paraphrase of the work of early 20th century, Swiss born psychologist Karl Gustav Jung. He wrote this brilliant loophole to this question in his book *Answer to Job*, his commentary on the Biblical book of Job.

I'm not quite certain that his line of thinking would be my exact reasoning; nonetheless, I want to share (or at least summarize) it.

What Jung said was that God is not fully conscious of God's self! Consequently, God created creatures that could be capable of consciousness to help inform God as to what God is really like. And that self awareness is really what God wants.

For me, I don't really know why God would want or need things of us.

Very studious, serious theologians and philosophers require consistency of themselves when they write about God and/or reality.

I'm neither.

My logical argument and cogent reasoning ducks don't align perfectly — and I'm all right with that. I can't "prove" why God wants more love in the world — all I know is that it is true: God wants more love in the world.

I'm all right with that.

# YOUR OWN THEOPHANY

## FINDING OUT WHAT (THE) GOD (OF YOUR UNDERSTANDING) WANTS FROM YOU.

I'm going to present three different ways of getting your own answers to the question of what it is that God — howsoever you might understand the word — might want from you.

    1) A Simple Spiritual-Religious Exercise

    2) Prayer

    3) Role-playing

The first is a simple, spiritual-religious exercise that will take no more than 10 minutes. The second is prayer, which will make more sense when I've explained what prayer actually is. The third is a bit more psychological and involves some role-playing.

# A SIMPLE SPIRITUAL-RELIGIOUS EXERCISE

On the next pages will be a few tasks geared towards your finding at least one (and most probably more than one) notion of what (the) God (of your understanding) might want from you.

No matter what you do or don't believe regarding organized religion, the Bible, and/or God, this spiritual-religious exercise will work.

But it will only work if you are willing to bring two things: a willingness to participate and some time to be willing. (You need about 10 minutes.)

## TIME TRAVEL #1: GOING BACK

You have exactly five minutes from the time you read these words to finish the following exercise. No stalling, just do it. (It's actually plenty of time and the exercise is not too hard.)

Picture yourself at your current age — right now, where you are, doing exactly what you are doing. Reading these words. Breathing. Thinking.

> Think about yourself at your current age minus 10-25 years. How old were you? _____.

Think about some spiritual-religious advice that you wished you, 10-25 years ago, could have benefited from hearing from you now, 10-25 years wiser than you were then.

Now imagine you are giving your past self that wisdom.

Examples of spiritual-religious (or general attitudinal) advice are *be grateful* or *accept more love*.

Keep these four things in mind:

> 1) You have four minutes from this very moment to be done with this part.
>
> 2) You cannot give yourself any spiritual-religious wisdom that would cause you not to be exactly where you are right now.
>
> 3) You are only allowed to write a maximum of 3 lines. (And, although I promote religion-outside-the-box, I'm going to ask you to stay within the box here.)
>
> 4) Be warned: this exercise has been known to bring up powerful emotions.

Write some spiritual-religious wisdom or advice you think you would have benefited from knowing 10-25 years ago.

(For example, the first time I did this exercise I wrote, "Relax a little, God is present.")

---

Spiritual-religious advice from me at age ____ (current age) to me at ____ years old (age 10-25 years ago):

_____

_____

_____

---

Good.

When you are finished, take a deep, cleansing breath.

## Time Travel #2:
## Going Ahead

Now we are ready to bump it up a notch.

Take another breath.
(Reminder: exhaling is part of a full breath!)

You have exactly five minutes to do the following exercise.

> Think about yourself at your current age plus 10-25 years. How old will you be? _____ .

Think about the spiritual-religious advice your future self (living 10-25 years into the future) would give to your present self today.

Let's look at it this way: if you continue on the trajectory your life is on, you will probably be wiser in 10-25 years than you are today. Assuming that's true, what spiritual-religious advice would that wiser version of you want you to have now, as you read these words today?

Again, you have a maximum of three lines and just under five minutes from this moment to finish. Do not procrastinate.

Think about it. Give it a few moments for a phrase to come to you. When you find that phrase, please write it down.

(The quote I came up with the first time I did this was: "Don't be afraid to shine!")

> Spiritual-religious advice from me at age _____
> (age 10-25 years in the future) to me at _____
> years old (current age):
>
> _____
>
> _____
>
> _____

When you are finished, take another deep, cleansing breath (or a sigh).

## Putting it All Together

If everything went according to plan, you should have some really good spiritual-religious advice on the preceeding lines.

And this spiritual-religious advice is personal to you.

Wonderful!

Take a look at what you wrote.

There might be some overlap between what you wrote to your past self and what your future self wrote to you. And, that's not unusual — it's the same you, after all.

On the other hand, there might not be overlap. That can be really interesting, too. Many people will give their past self advice that is more active than what it is their future self instructs them.

(Why? It is much easier to say, "I wish I had _____ __" instead of starting the process now. It's easier to blame and regret than to be proactive and responsible.)

This putting-it-together is really difficult. Look at the bits of spiritual-religious advice to yourself. Find *one* important idea or theme and see if you can't boil that whole thing down to one, two, three, four, or five words — a notion of what it is that (the) God (of your understanding) wants from you.

Write your theophany — *what (the) God (of your understanding) Wants From You* — here:

_____

_____

_____

# PRAYER

Prayer is often assumed to be the proper means for contacting and receiving messages from God. And, you can use prayer to divine what (the) God (of your understanding) wants. Unfortunately, there is a lot that needs to be unlearned and relearned about prayer for that to make sense.

But before we analyze what prayer is, should be and how we can do it properly, here is my favorite joke about prayer:

> A man driving, late for an important meeting, can't find a parking spot. He circles the block, curses his timing, then decides to pray, "God, if you give me a parking spot, I'll turn my life around." Just then, he sees the perfect parking spot, exactly in front of him. "Never mind, God," he says, "I got one."

There are three types of prayers:

1) Petition prayers

2) Praise prayers

3) Presence prayers

## Petition Prayer

The derivation of the English word "prayer" might be partly to blame for the fact that we usually think of prayer as petition. "Prayer" comes from the Latin *precari* — "to request."

Scientists are on both sides of the "efficacy of petition prayer" debate. Some seem certain that prayer affects reality, while others are certain that prayer does not affect reality. (Certainty means that you are certain, not that you're right or wrong.)

There are double-blind studies showing that mold, when "prayed for," grows faster than mold that has not been prayed for. And, there have been double-blind studies in which mold, when "prayed for" doesn't grow faster.

Moreover, believing that petition prayers get answered leads to theological problems: 1) What happens when what you ask for isn't delivered? 2) Is prosperity synonymous with God's favor?

The usual answer to the first question can feel like the wool is being pulled over your eyes: God did answer, but chose — for a wiser reason, obviously — not to grant what was wished for. We can easily understand why a parent wouldn't give a toddler poison no matter how much the child begged for it. But, this logic doesn't hold water with other adult examples like disease and genocide.

The only answer I like to the second question is something I heard said by Dan-the-God-Man, a street preacher: "You can tell the people who God has blessed because they have a smile on their face." God's blessings aren't material things.

Petition prayer is asking for something from (the) God (of your understanding).

## Praise Prayer

The purpose of praise prayers is to shout out a commendation to God and to acknowledge how good we have it. "How blessed are we," is an example of the beginning of a praise prayer.

So are gratitude lists. (Incidentally, the health benefits of gratitude lists are pretty incontrovertible.)

The coolest thing about a well-formed praise prayer is the little high you get after reciting it. At the risk of being a pusher, let me suggest that we try one now.

I want you to notice your mood now before we start.

As you fill in the blanks on the next page, watch what happens to your mood and attitude. Keep in mind that your mood is *supposed* to spike upwards a little. This doesn't always happen, so watch to see what happens for you in this moment.

- I am joyful that I can

_____

_____

_____


- I am glad that I have

_____

_____

_____


- I am thankful for

_____

_____

_____

Are the blanks filled in? Good. You have just written three praise prayers.

(If you want extra-credit, see if you can answer the same three questions but this time using the word God. I thank God that I can _____, I thank God that I have _____, I thank God for _____. Raising the bar even higher, try these: Thank you, God, that I can _____, thank you, God, that I have _____, thank you, God, for _____.)

Creating a gratitude list is a wonderful thing to do right before falling asleep and immediately upon waking up. Such a list reminds you of things you have and are grateful for, as opposed to what you are scared of and lacking.

Moreover, the attitude of gratitude is contagious and is said to attract good things.

Praise prayer is thanking (the) God (of your understanding).

## Presence Prayer

The truest form of prayer is this last type of prayer: the prayer of being present.

Presence prayer is the hands down best way of contacting and receiving contact from God — however you choose to understand God.

Before we get into that, let me ask you: Have you ever found yourself blabbing on someone's voicemail? You're just talking without realizing what you are saying. It comes out as a live stream of subconscious rambling. You think you're being concise but then realize you were just spewing out words?

That free flowing experience is similar to the true form of a present prayer, minus the answering machine.

Think about any good soliloquy, which occurs when a character is torn over what to do. The character feels troubled, but in the course of talking through their problems, they attain some resolution.

A soliloquy might be an act of "experiencing conscious contact with a Higher Power" or "being present in life as it unfolds." Or it could be "an act of attempting to contact (the) God (of your understanding)." A presence prayer is the feeling of having spent a few moments in God's presence. It's somewhat conscious, somewhat unconscious — and never goes exactly the way you thought it would go.

Presence prayer — conscious contact with God — is not about feeling good or asking for things. It's about being present. It's about being in the here and now. It's not asking God to change anything. It's not thanking God or thinking. It's just being.

Here are a few of my favorite quotes about this real kind of prayer:

> Prayer is not asking. It is a longing of the soul.
> It is daily admission of one's weakness... It is

> better in prayer to have a heart without words than words without a heart. -*Mohandas Gandhi*
>
> Prayer does not change God, but it changes the one who prays. -*Sören Kierkegaard*
>
> The issue of prayer is not prayer; the issue of prayer is God. -*Abraham Joshua Heschel*

Real prayers of presence require humility and surrender.

Humility is saying, "I am not enough. I need help. I cannot do it alone. I do not know what will happen." It takes humility to go to this place of helplessness and unknowing. Surrender is linked to this. It's knowing that the answer you receive — while it might not be one you wanted to hear — might be the real answer.

Finally, there is one more quote I want to share. It's one of my favorite quotes in the world. It is a quote from Tayfur Abu Yazid Al-Bistami, the 9th century Persian Sufi. This marvelous quote speaks to humility, surrender, and the nature of presence prayer.

> For years, I would say, 'Do this' and 'Give me that.' When I reached the shores of wisdom, I said, 'God, be mine and do what You want.'

Presence prayers are about being where you are, when you are there.

I find toddlers to be wonderful role models for being present in life as it happens. They are unconstrained by the adult worry of what others will think of them.

In my opinion, when you are here — and just doing what you are supposed to be doing — that is a most beautiful presence prayer.

(You don't need to believe in an active, external God to understand what I'm saying here. Of course, you might and you can, but you don't have to.)

For presence prayer to happen, we need to carve out some space. We must create a safe space where we don't feel like we have to get all the words right, and where we can allow ourselves to tolerate our humanity. In this safe place, we can tolerate the mistakes we've made in our lives. If we do not create a space containing these qualities, transformation is not likely.

Accordingly, there are far fewer "suppose to's" involved with praying a presence prayer than you probably thought. Hands clasped together or eyes closed are not requirements. (Rumor has it that they aren't even required for petition and praise prayers.)

The following truth about prayer is one I like a lot: *You don't even have to like your prayer.*

It's just about you attempting contact with God; no promise you'll connect or even like it.

Here are my step-by-step suggestiongs on how to pray a presence prayer:

## How to Pray

- Start out by naming God with whatever name you choose to name that which cannot be named: "Higher Power," "HaShem," "Jesus," "Allah," "Goddess," "Jehovah," "Tao," "Mother," etc. You don't have to always use the same name, either.
- Pause.
- Using your active mind, do a quick survey of how you feel, giving attention to your physical body, your thoughts, and your emotions.
- Breathe.
- Repeat the name you've chosen for God.
- Make a few full sentences in your heart or aloud, directed outside of your self.
- Pause.
- Breathe.
- Optional: say, "Amen."

(Amen is said to be related to the Hebrew root word for "faith." It is customarily said as an expression of agreement at the end of a prayer.)

I will ask you in a moment to try this.

It might not feel like something you want to do. And you might have some good reasons why you wouldn't, shouldn't, or don't want to.

Hey, I grew up in a culturally Jewish household and got the impression that prayers to God should be in Hebrew, from a book, and only said at their proper times. Rabbinical school furthered in me the notion that prayers were non-English, non-spontaneous, and time sensitive. I know how awkward this can feel.

I understand that if you have never improvised or said a presence prayer, it may feel awkward.

Furthermore, if part of your self-image includes the notion that you're not the type of person who prays (granted that you didn't know what prayer was really about when you set that rule), this exercise will probably feel exceptionally weird.

On the positive side, why would you *not* want to try this?

Let me tell you what you have to gain: a sense of yourself, a sense of your relationship to (the) God (of your understanding), possibly both, and perhaps some notion of what it is that God — howsoever you might understand that word — might want from you.

So, let's give it a whirl right now:

- Name God.
- Pause.
- Survey yourself physically, emotionally, and mentally.
- Breathe.
- Rename God.
- Say a few things.
- Pause.
- Breathe.
- Optional: say, "Amen."

Amen.

# ROLE-PLAYING

This last technique we will use to find out what (the) God (of your understanding) wants from you is the most powerful one we will do.

It involves a bit of role-playing.

Do not skip doing this or just read the words, *do this exercise*!

If you need a break, take one now and then come back to this when you can dedicate 20 minutes to read and do this. (It will probably take you less time, but let's be safe.)

And, you've got to be in the right place before you do this role-playing. What is on the next pages can bring up some really strong emotions. If you aren't in a place physically, emotionally or mentally to go there, don't do this now. (I know for some, not being in a "safe" place to do this would unconsciously be a benefit — this way you have an excuseas to why you can't go deep. Of course, you are really only short-changing yourself, but do what you have to.)

### SET UP.

During this role-playing, there will be three questions and three roles.

## Questions

After you've answered the first question, move along to the second question. No rush. And then, when you feel ready, the third question.

(Do not do the second question — or even read it — until you have completed the first. And, similarly, complete your answer to the second before you even read the third.)

## Roles

There will be three parts in this role-playing. We will switch parts some, but for now, these are the parts and who is playing each of them.

> **You.** You will be playing the part of you. So, just be yourself. (Congratulations, you're a natural.)

> **Rabbi Brian.** I will be playing my part — an attentive and compassionate listener. My role is a blend of compassionate clergyman, couple's therapist, and spiritual director.*

---

\* Many people do not know about spiritual direction. Here is a quote explaining what we do from the web site of Spiritual Directors International — a group of which I am a member: *Spiritual direction is the process of accompanying people on a spiritual journey. Spiritual direction helps people tell their sacred stories every day. Spiritual direction exists in a context that emphasizes growing closer to God (or the holy or a higher power). Spiritual direction invites a deeper relationship with the spiritual aspect of being human. Spiritual direction is not psychotherapy, counseling, or financial planning to help people in their search for meaning and connection to God.*

**God.** The third part is going to be played by God. (You'll see.)

## Question One.

Rabbi Brian:

> Before I ask the first question, I want to make certain you understand why we are here. To quote one of my favorite artists, who is again known as Prince, "We are gathered here today to get through this thing called life." That's why we are here.
>
> And, let me welcome you.
>
> We are here in this counseling session of sorts to clear the air a bit.
>
> It seems without noticing it, in this relationship — the one between you and God — some cleaning needs to be done. Some things seem to have been brushed under the proverbial rug, other assumptions have remained unspoken for quite some time, and it is my hope that with some exploration, some clarity might be attained.
>
> This is a relationship and no real relationship is stagnant. Dialogue is a way to see where things are, and that's what we are here to do — enter into some dialogue.

What is said here stays here and doesn't need to be shared with anyone else. And, what is said here is just about the here and now — it's nothing to be carved in stone and held as true for all time.

We are going to start with God just listening, and you responding to the first question.

This all being said, let's all take a breath, and begin.

My first question is — and please be honest in your answer — do you feel awkward, odd, set up, etc., that, when you boil it down, you find yourself in what amounts to a therapy session with God?

<u>You:</u>

How I feel finding myself in what amounts to a therapy session with God...

_____

_____

_____

_____

_____

_____

_____

# Question Two.

Rabbi Brian:

> Now let us move to question number two.
>
> The set-up will be the same: God listening, you answering.
>
> Here's the question: "What complaints, grievances, grudges etc. do you have about your recent relationship with God?"
>
> In other words, what is it that you have not said to God that you know deep in your heart you want to say about your relationship as of late? It might be something that you haven't felt particularly safe to say or just something you haven't had the opportunity to say.
>
> Or it might just be something that bears repeating that you've said before.
>
> I would advise that you start somewhere and give yourself permission to just go from there — not exactly certain of where you are going to wind up. (Amazing things might just come out.)
>
> Do at least 7 sentences. There is no one who can't do that. (Even if you claim to have no relationship with God, that's a starting point.)
>
> And, I would like to specify here that if you would like to answer about earlier times in

your life, you can and do so later. For right now, please focus on what's troubling you in your recent and/or current relationship with God.

Thank you.

You:

Complaints, grievances, grudges, etc., I have about my recent and/or current relationship with God. (At least 7 sentences.)

_____
_____
_____
_____
_____
_____
_____
_____
_____
_____
_____
_____
_____

*Complaints, grievances, grudges, etc., about my current and/or recent relationship with God ... (continued)*

## QUESTION THREE.

Make certain you have completed your answers for the two preceding questions before continuing.

Really.

Now to prepare for the third question, we are going to have a change in roles.

God now is going to play your part and you, the reader, are now going to play God's part. That is, you will now answer on behalf of God. (I will remain in my role.)

At this time, I will ask God (being played by you) to answer and you (being played by God) to remain silent and listen attentively.

Rabbi Brian:

> What complaints, grievances, etc., do you, God, have about your relationship with the reader? What is it you want the reader to know, but for whatever reasons, you have been unable to voice recently?
> 
> I will ask you to not go tit-for-tat or to defend yourself based on what just happened. Certainly, that will be a part of what is going on, but the focus should be what you, God, find lacking, difficult, etc., about this current relationship. (Again, this is not the time to delve into things from a long time ago — for

right now, please focus on what's wrong with this current relationship.)

I will ask you, God, to start writing somewhere and see where that leads...shoot for a minimum of 3 paragraphs.

God:

What is lacking, difficult, etc. about my current relationship with the reader.... (At least 3 paragraphs.)

_____
_____
_____
_____
_____
_____
_____
_____
_____
_____
_____
_____

*What is lacking, difficult, etc. about my (God's) current relationship with the reader…. (continued)*

# Review.

> Please do not read this review unless you have done the three parts of the above exercise. If you haven't written at least a few paragraphs in answering questions two and three, please do so before moving on.
>
> Thanks.

Obviously, I don't know what it is you wrote down either as you or as God.

Consequently, I can't give you detailed information in this review.

What I can tell you is that some people do feel tweaked right after having done this — and that's normal and makes sense. If you just let yourself write, you might have been a bit surprised to find yourself expressing some of the things that you did. And for some people, some really strong emotions surfaced — and it can feel a little odd to have strong emotions come up in a setting like this.

Then there is the time delay. If you are reading this immediately after having done the exercise, you might not feel much of anything at all. That's quite normal and to be expected. What's also normal but not always expected is what will happen in a week when you re-read what you wrote — when there is some time between you and what you wrote, you might see things you didn't expect to see.

So, I advise that you think about your answers now and then sit on your answers for a little while. Then, in a week, re-read what you wrote and reflect back. Chances are, there is something that will strike you as a bit surprising.

Look at the tone of what you wrote. The tone with which you wrote to God might have been snotty or ingratiating. And, you might find that the tone with which you wrote as God was the same tone that you would use to speak to a disobedient child. What tone did you use in each case?

Also, think about talking this out with another human being. You can get a friend who will promise to just look you in the eyes and not say anything as you talk or, better yet, find a spiritual director, clergy person, or therapist.

Call any church, synagogue, or mosque and tell them that you want to talk to someone about your relationship with God — the people who work there will be more than happy to talk with you — and not in some spooky way. This is what clergy folk, for the most part, love to talk about, really. Why else do you think they are working in a church, synagogue, or mosque? (It might take you a few calls before you find someone you are comfortable talking with, but it's time worth investing.)

If you want to find a spiritual director, take a look at www.sdiworld.org.

# (RABBI BRIAN'S ANSWERS)

You don't have to read this section.

Really.

You can skip it.

You've already gotten a lot of answers of what it is that God wants from you and this section mainly contains a catalogue of those things that I have come to realize that God wants from me.

I'm sharing this list of things that I know in my heart of hearts I'm supposed to be doing — hopefully — to inspire you in you finding your own.

Accordingly, at the end of each of my sections is a place for you to write your thoughts. (You'll see.) So feel free to take from my writing any bits that work for you — underline, star, highlight the things you like. Cross out what you don't like.

And, then compile your list.

Where our lists overlap, hooray!

Where our lists diverge, hooray!

When it comes to your list, if you are weirded out by the notion of "I know (the) God (of my understanding) wants me to...," you can substitute "I know I need to..." or "This is a spiritual-religious goal for my life...."

My answers will be in two parts: (1) Short answers of one or two sentences. (2) Longer, essay-type answers.

And, so you can expect it, some parts of the answers overlap.

## Short answers:

**Be.** God wants me to stop dwelling in the past and the future, to just be where I am. And, God reminds me as I lose my way again and again, it is always simpler than I remember.

**Celebrate freedom.** God wants me to relax, enjoy, and celebrate what I can.

**Confidence.** God wants me to remember that my opinion of what I am doing is much more important than anyone else's opinion.

**Creativity.** God would rather me create a prayer — a painting, a lyric, a tear — than re-hash a centuries old rote one.

**Free myself.** God wants me to free myself from my false notions of me: that I am what I do, what I think, what I have, or what I feel.

**Kindness.** God wants me to act toward others and myself with kindness.

**Know myself.** God wants me to know who I am so that I can get a clearer perspective on reality. "Whoever knows him or herself knows God." (Muhammad)

**Live outside my head.** God wants me to get out of my head, more into my heart, freer.

**Passion.** God wants me to pursue life with passion — even when I am mourning or anxious — and to do everything with a full heart.

**Relax.** God wants me to feel like I'm away for the weekend enjoying rather than stressing out about things.

**Surrender.** God wants me to surrender, to let go and let God steer without being an obnoxious, smarter-than-the-driver passenger.

## Your turn:

Now, write some of your short answers on the lines that follow.

> - You can substitute "I know I need to" or "I ought to" for "(The) God (of my understanding) wants me to."
>
> - Don't skimp! The amount of time you spend writing your answers is worth at least double the amount of time you spend thinking about your answers and quadruple the amount of time you spent reading my answers.
>
> - Take a little peak in the deepest part of your heart and you might find another answer or two there.

## Short answers:

(The) God (of my understanding) wants me to:

_____
_____
_____
_____

(The) God (of my understanding) wants me to:

_____
_____
_____
_____
_____

(The) God (of my understanding) wants me to:

_____
_____
_____
_____
_____

(The) God (of my understanding) wants me to:

_____
_____
_____
_____
_____

(The) God (of my understanding) wants me to:

_____
_____
_____
_____

(The) God (of my understanding) wants me to:

_____
_____
_____
_____

(The) God (of my understanding) wants me to:

_____
_____
_____
_____

(The) God (of my understanding) wants me to:

_____
_____
_____
_____
_____

(The) God (of my understanding) wants me to:

_____
_____
_____
_____
_____

(The) God (of my understanding) wants me to:

_____
_____
_____
_____
_____

(The) God (of my understanding) wants me to:

_____
_____
_____
_____

(The) God (of my understanding) wants me to:

_____
_____
_____
_____

(The) God (of my understanding) wants me to:

_____
_____
_____
_____

## Longer, essay-type answers:

These are my longer, essay-type answers to the question of what God wants from me. Mark up the text and the margins with your notes, corrections, etc. The chance for you to add your own comments to each of the topics I have chosen will follow each of my sections. And, then after my last section, there will be some pages for you to put in your longer, essay-type answers that I don't touch on at all.

- Acceptance.

- A Relationship with Me.

- Be Where I Am.

- Love.

- Shine.

- Stuff.

## Acceptance.

Late 13th and early 14th century mystic Meister Eckhart said, "God wants nothing of you but the gift of a peace-filled heart."

This is true. God wants my heart to be peace filled.

This, I have learned, is not the same as happiness.

There is a notion on the street that God wants you to be happy all the time. That's simply not right. (You might, after taking your spiritual-religious life into your own hands, feel more peace filled, but that's not the same as happy.) God wants me to have a peace-filled heart, to experience all the emotions of a filled life, not for me to be constantly strung out on or looking for a hit of the drug "happiness."

(Happy is a dangerous goal. "Happy" is a relative term, and therefore it both has limits and is momentary. The pursuit of constant happiness and its inevitable failure, however, does drive much of the U.S. economy.)

Peace isn't just the absence of strife — it's the harmony of the apparently disharmonious. A peace-filled heart is one that can contain in harmony the apparently disharmonious — happy and sad, love and hate, good and bad.

As a child, I used to fervently strive to see *only* the happy, to the point of denying "negative" emotions and imagining a "happy island" that someday I would reach. I'm wiser now to know that within each joy there is sadness — for example, at every wedding there is a cause for celebration that the couple found each other and there is also, while hardly ever acknowledged, a sadness that they will have to lose each other. I know now that there is a shadow side to every positive emotion and that God wants my heart to be filled, not delusional.

God wants me to be present to reality, accepting and experiencing reality as it is. To accept the things I cannot change, even if I don't like them. To exist in the world, as it is, right now, wholly.

Acceptance is not abetting, advocating, agreeing, aiding, approving, assisting, authenticating, authorizing, backing, complying, concurring, confirming, consenting, cultivating, encouraging, endorsing, furthering, liking, maintaining, permitting, promoting, ratifying, reinforcing, sanctifying, supporting, or sympathizing. Acceptance is saying, "It is what it is, and what it is, is what is."

Jane, my wife, once defined true happiness for a class I was teaching with the following:

> Happiness is not things going or coming your way, but being in a relationship with reality.

That's it. Taking reality as it is, accepting it. Exactly what Eckhart said, but in different words.

We can also sing it with the Beatles's wording and melody, "Let it be."

This truth is repackaged over and over and over again, in every language, and at least once a generation, one form of it becomes a hit. It's the crux of the current-day bestsellers "The Power of Now" and "Loving What Is." And, there's reason to say it over and over again: it's a truth, like a songbird or anything holy, that cannot be held in captivity and maintain its radiance.

Ram Dass, the 1970s iconoclast and guru, said it in three words, "Be Here Now."

The truth is that this, right here, right now, is the only reality. Now. Here. Not hoping that anything will be different, but just being here with a peace-filled heart.

Lamenting, regretting, and living in the past is a denial of the splendor of the present. Fearing and overly preparing for the future does the same. We need to understand something that 17th century philosopher Benedict Spinoza said: "Reality and perfection are synonymous."

With a theological bent to it, Eckhart said the same:

> You might ask, "How can I know if something is God's will?" My answer is, "If it were not God's will, it wouldn't exist even for an instant; so if something happens, it must be God's will."

If we accept that reality is exactly as it is — then accepting that reality is exactly synonymous with God's will isn't a far leap at all.

Let me end with the rest of the above Eckhart quote:

> If you truly enjoyed God's will, you would feel exactly as though you were in the kingdom of

heaven, whatever happened to you or didn't happen to you.

## Thoughts On Acceptance.

With regard to acceptance, (the) God (of my understanding) wants:

_____
_____
_____
_____
_____
_____
_____
_____
_____
_____
_____
_____
_____
_____
_____
_____
_____

## A RELATIONSHIP WITH ME.

Rabbi Abraham Joshua Heschel — considered by many to be one of the most significant Jewish theologians of the 20th century — wrote that society's problems were not caused by humanity seeking and searching for God. He wrote that the ills stemmed from God searching for humanity and humanity making excuses, running away.

Nineteenth century Polish scholar Menachem Mendel of Kotzk once asked a group of students, as the introduction to a longer discussion, "Where is God?" The students' answered his softball question with words they knew by heart: *God is everywhere.* (Although, in the way I initially heard the story, they put it in a bit more Biblical language, "The whole earth is filled with God's glory."[*]) The great teacher exclaimed, "No! God is only where humanity makes room for God."

Carl Jung had the Latin phrase *Vocatus Atque Non Vocatus Deus Aderit* (Invited or not invited, God is present) inscribed above his doorway.

I often run away from, fail to make space for, and ignore God.

God is in the present all around me right this moment. And, as with a faint star in the heavens, as soon as I stare at it, it disappears; God, likewise, is really hard to keep an eye on.

---

[*] Numbers 14:21.

God, as I understand it, wants a relationship with me. A real one. A present day one. Not one based on the fact that I'm circumcised or that I was ordained as a rabbi. Not one based in history, but one based right here and now in the here and now. God wants to be a part of my life, even if that means a few more sessions of us going to couple's counseling.

The God of my understanding doesn't want me to have blind devotion. God wants to wrestle with me and for us to proverbially enjoy a glass of schnapps together.

God wants me to be in a relationship — a real, adult-type relationship. The type in which I can tell God honestly, as I do with my wife and closest friends, when I feel disappointed or annoyed in the way I feel I'm being treated.

God, I am certain now, was glad when I wrote a Dear John letter to officially break-up and that I taught a class entitled "God is dead and I don't feel too good myself" because I was working on our relationship — not ignoring it, but working through the difficult parts. God wanted then and still wants from me some inkling of where our relationship stands.

Like it or not, God is here, all around me, and God wants to be more a part of my life.

## Thoughts on a Relationship With God.

With regard to my relationship with (the) God (of my understanding), (the) God (of my understanding) wants:

_____
_____
_____
_____
_____
_____
_____
_____
_____
_____
_____
_____
_____
_____
_____
_____
_____
_____
_____
_____

## Be where I am.

The other day, when I got back from exercising, I was greeted by 30 e-mails requiring answers, three voicemails, four bills needing payment, about 15 minutes of paperwork related to the non-profit status of Religion-Outside-The-Box, and this book…which at that time needed a bunch more work.

I suddenly found myself overcome by an overwhelming feeling of anxiety. It felt as though I was choking.

"Suck it up," I told myself.

But what would battening down the hatches accomplish?

It would suffocate me, stuffing the scared feeling down while I robotically muscled through my responsibilities.

I knew from experience that ignoring my anxiety would just wreak havoc later in incalculable ways.

So, I decided to try something different: I wrote God a prayer for help.

I didn't write to God because I expected God to change things for me — I had already written the section on prayer and knew that's not how prayer works. I wrote it because I know that when we engage in real earnest prayer, the one who prays is changed.

Five paragraphs into my stream-of-consciousness-prayer, a favorite Robert Frost quote came to mind: "The best way out is always through" and I muttered and mumbled it aloud. A thought occurred to me, "What if I embrace just my feelings? Why not just sit with the panic…lean into it?"

So, I did.

I placed the fleshy part of my palm on my cheeks, my fingers covering my eyes. I bowed my head toward my chest, and I cried. I wept. I dove into the feelings. I allowed my panic and fear to wash over me.

To my amazement, it didn't last forever. In reality, it lasted all of 40 seconds.

Then, looking like a two-year-old who has just finished a tantrum — with tears still damp on my cheeks — I felt my countenance lift. The feelings of panic had disappeared.

God wants me to feel sad when I am sad, to feel angry when I am angry, to feel overwhelmed when I am overwhelmed, to feel happy when I am happy.

Not to be sad, angry, overwhelmed or happy according to any notion of "how I think I am supposed to be" any of those things, but to just be it as I am in it.

## Thoughts about being where I am:

With regard to my being where I am, (the) God (of my understanding) wants:

_____
_____
_____
_____
_____
_____
_____
_____
_____
_____
_____
_____
_____
_____
_____
_____
_____
_____

## Love.

God wants me to love others, to love myself, and to love God.

As modern comedian (and preacher) George Carlin put it, "Why does religion tell us to love others, love yourself, and love God? That's because it's all the same thing!" (It gets a big laugh the way he says it. Truth is often very funny.)

God wants me to love people as they are, not as I would like them to be. (The horrible opposite of loving someone is ignoring and not seeing them as they are.)

God wants me to love myself exactly how I am. Not to think that I am less than whole or that I am defective.

God wants me to love the world how it is. (Or at the very least accept how it is and to try to stop fighting it so much.)

Moreover, God wants me to accept love.

Although it is sometimes human nature to feel more comfortable "guilty" than "forgiven" or "loved," I am called upon to feel the love. When people give me compliments, I ought not play those down. I ought to take in the love.

God wants me to know that God loves me. God wants me to shake myself free of all the things that entangle me and God wants me to know that I am both loved and accepted.

Sometimes, I feel that if I accept God's love, then there would be strings attached — that I would have to do some things differently. I know, at least on paper, that God loves me exactly how I am and that this isn't the case.

God loves me unconditionally — exactly as I am, warts, foibles, and all.

And, God wants me to feel loved.

I know God wants me to incorporate more love into my life, both by being loving and by being loved.

Thoughts on Love:

With regard to love, (the) God (of my understanding) wants:

_____

_____

_____

_____

_____

_____

_____

_____

## Shine.

God wants me to shine.

Godliness is within and can shine from inside of me to add sparkle and light to the world. (The Bible's creation story tells us that God created humanity in the image of the divine — and, if we're not going with the notion that God physically looks like us, it means we have a godliness spark within us.)

My shining brings more God into the world.

When I ask myself the question, "Do I allow myself to shine?" I know I want to answer in the affirmative, but I also know that there is almost a panic that happens in my head, when I hear that question — that perhaps I'm not doing as good of a job as I should be. I know I should shine, it's just that I don't always do it as well as I know I can.

I know I'm shining when I see light reflected back to me in the eyes of people around me, when I feel a tingle of razzle-dazzle in my soul. And, I know I ought to dive into that feeling as opposed to snuffing it out.

To be honestly frank, I have a hard time allowing myself to dive into my feelings of being enthusiastic and excited — the hallmark feelings of shining.

I know there is not one set way to shine. The same 110 volts can bake cookies or sharpen pencils. (Such an odd analogy, I know.) Sometimes I shine in helping people, sometimes in not helping people; sometimes in saving money, sometimes in splurging; sometimes in being intellectual, sometimes in not being smart at all; sometimes in my exuberance and sometimes in the way I have a hard day.

When I shine, I feel open, lighter. I'm more relaxed. When I let myself shine, I'm more generous in all ways, I sleep better, I like being around people.

When I'm not shining, I close down and feel a bit more comfortable, familiar, and in control. When I am not shining, I tend to sulk and punish. And, sometimes, when I'm not shining, I do worse: I seem to delight in tarnishing other people's shine; somehow thinking that because I can do so makes me feel better.

As I know that God wants me to shine, I hereby recommit to shining more.

<u>Thoughts on Shining.</u>

With regard to shining, (the) God (of my understanding) wants:

_____

_____

_____

_____

_____

_____

## STUFF.

God wants me to have more stuff. God wants me to buy things, get a momentary high off of the purchase, hoard it, get attached to it, and then, when that high wears off, get more stuff.

God wants me to avoid general low levels of anxiety through rampant consumerism. The more stuff I have, the more knickknacks, bric-a-brac, and collectables, the more I know God loves me and the more God knows how much love I have in return.

God wants me to have the newest of everything, even if that means wasting resources. God wants me to feel good about myself by looking at all the things I have accumulated in my life and God wants to be proud of me for stockpiling.

Alright, I'm full of it. God doesn't care about stuff.

While we get confused about our sense of self and our sense of stuff, God doesn't.

<u>Thoughts on Stuff.</u>

With regard to stuff, (the) God (of my understanding) wants:

_____

_____

_____

## Add your own

With regard to _____,
(the) God (of my understanding) wants:

_____

_____

_____

_____

_____

_____

_____

_____

_____

_____

_____

_____

_____

_____

_____

_____

_____

_____

With regard to _____,
(the) God (of my understanding) wants:

_____
_____
_____
_____
_____
_____
_____
_____
_____
_____
_____
_____
_____
_____
_____
_____
_____
_____
_____
_____
_____

With regard to _____,
(the) God (of my understanding) wants:

_____
_____
_____
_____
_____
_____
_____
_____
_____
_____
_____
_____
_____
_____
_____
_____
_____
_____
_____
_____

With regard to _____,
(the) God (of my understanding) wants:

_____
_____
_____
_____
_____
_____
_____
_____
_____
_____
_____
_____
_____
_____
_____
_____
_____
_____
_____

With regard to _____,
(the) God (of my understanding) wants:

_____
_____
_____
_____
_____
_____
_____
_____
_____
_____
_____
_____
_____
_____
_____
_____
_____
_____

With regard to _____,
(the) God (of my understanding) wants:

_____
_____
_____
_____
_____
_____
_____
_____
_____
_____
_____
_____
_____
_____
_____
_____
_____
_____
_____
_____

With regard to _____,
(the) God (of my understanding) wants:

With regard to _____,
(the) God (of my understanding) wants:

_____

_____

_____

_____

_____

_____

_____

_____

_____

_____

_____

_____

_____

_____

_____

_____

_____

_____

With regard to _____,
(the) God (of my understanding) wants:

_____
_____
_____
_____
_____
_____
_____
_____
_____
_____
_____
_____
_____
_____
_____
_____
_____
_____
_____
_____

With regard to _____,
(the) God (of my understanding) wants:

_____
_____
_____
_____
_____
_____
_____
_____
_____
_____
_____
_____
_____
_____
_____
_____
_____
_____
_____
_____

# CONCLUSION

I wrote in the introduction that my role in helping you develop your spiritual-religious life was to be a guide and a friend — to metaphorically take your hand so that we could journey together.

Our journey together concludes for now.

But, this journey through life — trying to figure out our relationship with God, the universe, and ourselves — continues.

Thank you for being my companion.

I am honored.

If you want to learn more about **Religion-Outside-The-Box**, make a tax-deductible donation, or if you want to sign-up to receive **The 77% Weekly: a free, 40/52-week-a-year, spiritual-religious newsletter**[*] — visit rotb.org.

With love,

Rabbi Brian

---

[*] If you liked this book, you'll like *The 77% Weekly*.

## Upcoming Religion Outside The Box Book Titles:

- *How To Come To An Adult Relationship With (The) God (Of Your Understanding).*

- *The Bible, What It Is, What It Isn't, & What You Need To Know.*

- *Spiritual-Religious Exercises & Ponderables.*

www.religion-outside-the-box.com

# QUICK ORDER FORM

**E-mail orders:** orders@rotb.org

**Postal Orders:** Religion-Outside-The-Box / Suite 200 / 12840 Riverside Drive / North Hollywood, CA 91607.

Please send ___ copies of **How to Find Out What (the) God (of your understanding) Wants From You.**

Name: _____

Address: _____

City: _____ State: _____ Zip: _____

Telephone: _____

E-mail: _____

**Sales Tax:** Add $1.24 for each book shipped within CA.

**Shipping:** $4.60 for each multiple of up to five books.

**Web:** shop.rotb.org

# QUICK ORDER FORM

**E-mail orders:** orders@rotb.org

**Postal Orders:** Religion-Outside-The-Box / Suite 200 / 12840 Riverside Drive / North Hollywood, CA 91607.

Please send ___ copies of **How to Find Out What (the) God (of your understanding) Wants From You.**

Name: _____

Address: _____

City: _____ State: _____ Zip: _____

Telephone: _____

E-mail: _____

**Sales Tax:** Add $1.24 for each book shipped within CA.

**Shipping:** $4.60 for each multiple of up to five books.


**Web:** shop.rotb.org

# ABOUT RABBI BRIAN

**Brian Zachary Mayer,** an ordained rabbi, is the Founder and Chief Religious Officer of Religion-Outside-The-Box — an internet based rabbinate-ministry devoted to empowering adults find and be with (the) God (of their understanding).

Rabbi Brian's lectures, books, newsletters, and podcasts have helped 1,000's in coming to a more mature relationship with God and their spiritual-religious lives — no matter their history, their understanding, or lack of clarity with the term God.

He returns every summer to the magic camp on the East Coast he attended as a child, encouraging children to find the magic within them.

He and his family live in the Los Angeles area.

Visit him online at www.rotb.org

3052662

Made in the USA